Kids Can Draw
PIRATES

by Philippe Legendre

Walter Foster

© 2002 Groupe Fleurus-Mame, Paris.
Text on pages 4–24 © 2002 Walter Foster Publishing, Inc. All rights reserved.
Original title *J'apprends à dessiner les pirates,* © 2000 Groupe Fleurus-Mame, Paris.

Attention Parents and Teachers

All children can draw a circle, a square, or a triangle . . . which means that they can also learn to draw a captain, ship, or treasure chest! The KIDS CAN DRAW learning method is easy and fun. Children will learn a technique and a vocabulary of shapes that will form the basis for all kinds of drawing.

Pictures are created by combining geometric shapes to form a mass of volumes and surfaces. From this stage, children can give character to their sketches with straight, curved, or broken lines.

With just a few strokes of the pencil, a pirate scene will appear—and with the addition of color, the picture will be a real work of art!

The KIDS CAN DRAW method offers a real apprenticeship in technique and a first look at composition, proportion, shapes, and lines. The simplicity of this method ensures that the pleasure of drawing is always the most important factor.

About Philippe Legendre

French painter, engraver, and illustrator, Philippe Legendre also runs a school of art for children aged 6–14 years. Legendre frequently spends time in schools and has developed this method of learning so that all children can discover the artist within themselves.

Helpful Tips

1. Each picture is made up of simple geometric shapes, which are illustrated at the top of the left-hand page. This is called the **Vocabulary of Shapes.** Encourage children to practice drawing each shape before starting their pictures.

2. Suggest children use a pencil to do their sketches. This way, if they don't like a particular shape, they can just erase it and try again.

3. A dotted line indicates that the line should be erased. Have children draw the whole shape and then erase the dotted part of the line.

4. Once children finish their drawings, they can color them with crayons, colored pencils, or felt-tip markers. They may want to go over the lines with a black pencil or pen.

Now let's get started!

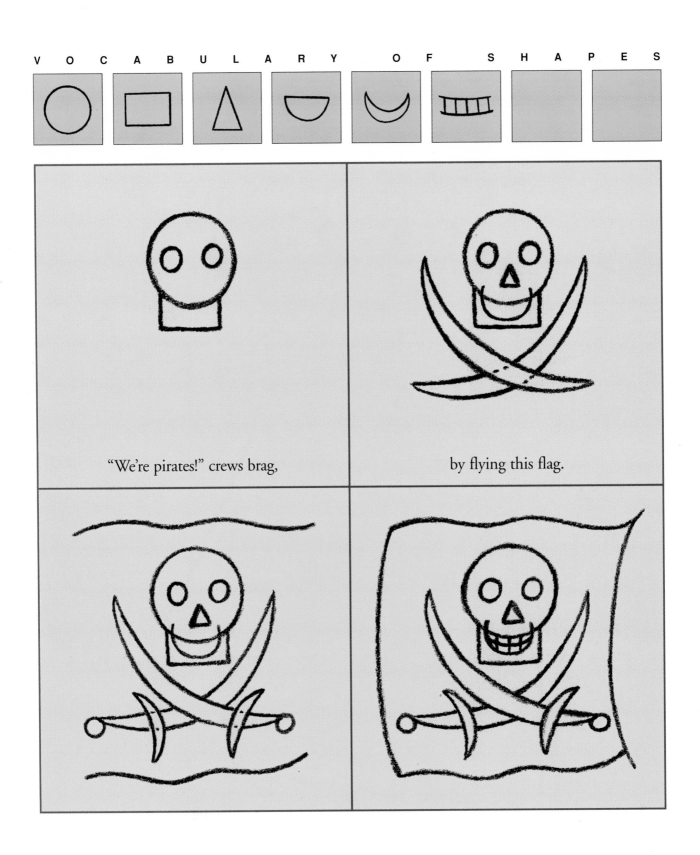

"We're pirates!" crews brag,

by flying this flag.

Jolly Roger

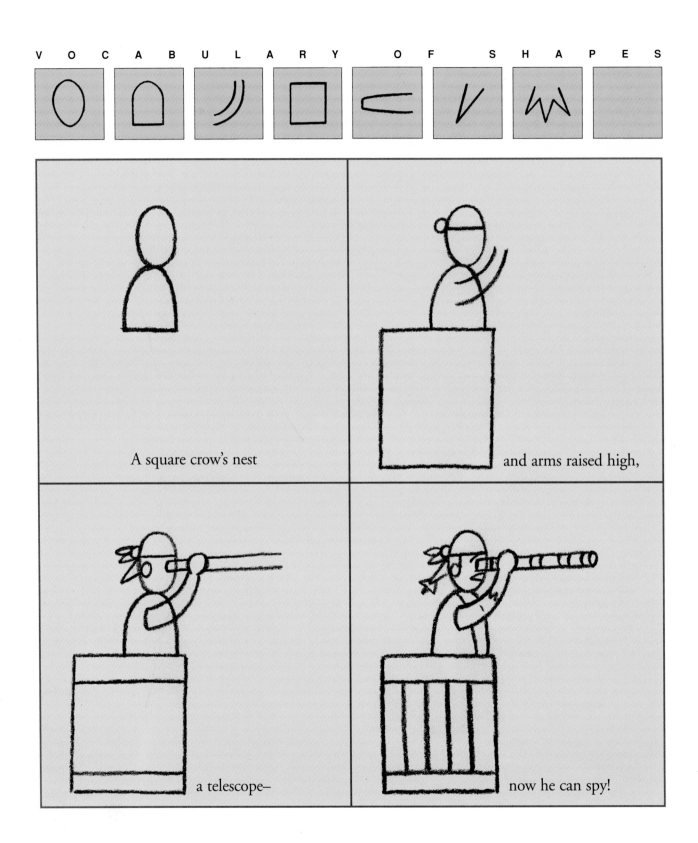

A square crow's nest

and arms raised high,

a telescope–

now he can spy!

Lookout

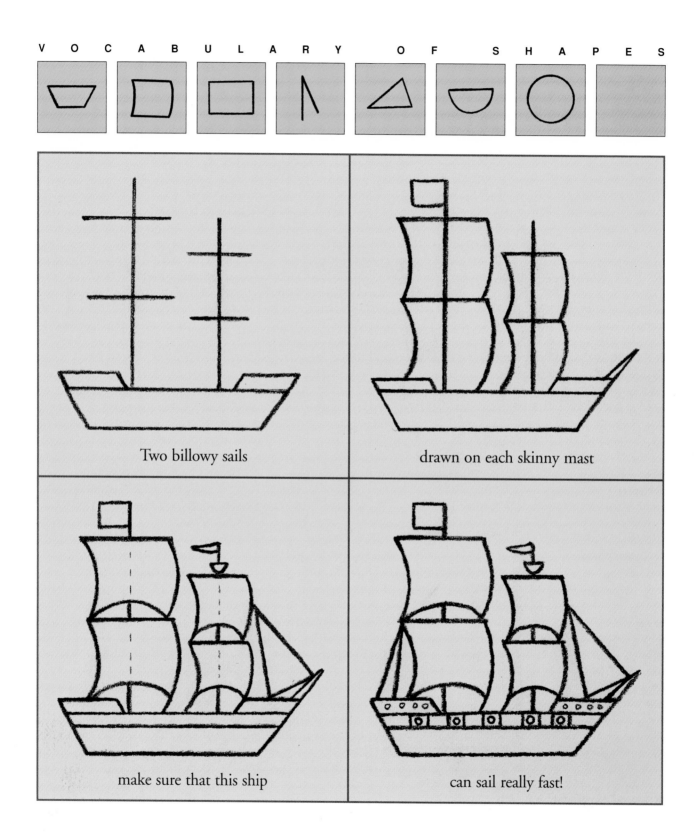

Two billowy sails

drawn on each skinny mast

make sure that this ship

can sail really fast!

Pirate Ship

Draw a hat on this crook,

then a sword and a hook.

Captain

The gruff pirate's wearing

a bird on his shoulder!

Draw a patch on his eye

so he looks even bolder.

Pirate

Arm the mad pirate

with pistol and sword.

His leg helps him float

if he falls overboard!

Pegleg

Draw a snarl and a beard

on the man sailors feared.

Blackbeard

Draw a round barrel

to keep him afloat.

He's facing a shark

and he hasn't a boat!

Castaway

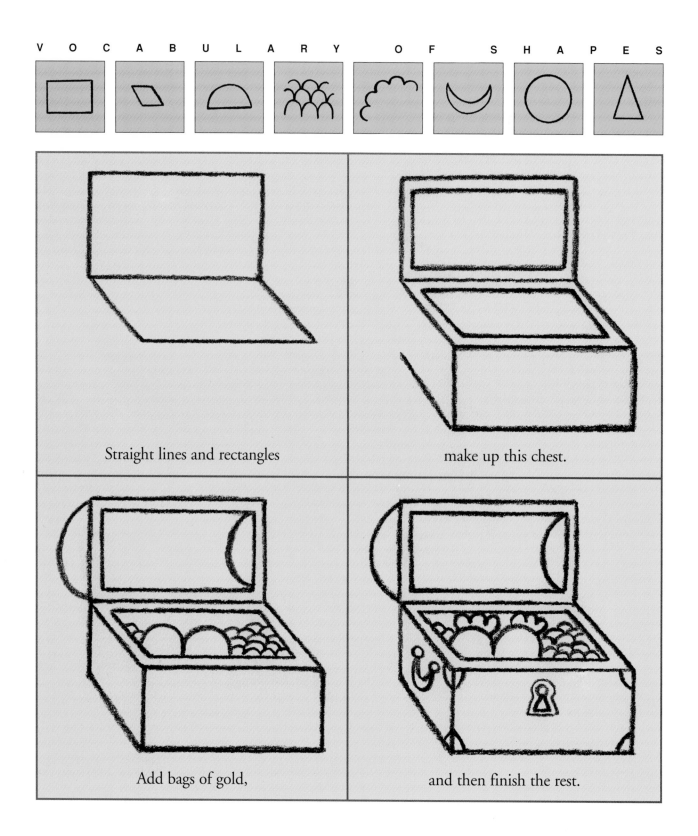

Straight lines and rectangles

make up this chest.

Add bags of gold,

and then finish the rest.

Treasure

The pirates have landed and found all the gold.

Now draw your own story for all to behold!